BEYOND THE CLASSROOM

A QUICK READ ABOUT STRIKING A BALANCE BETWEEN MAINSTREAM MENTALITY AND ONE'S INNER VOICE

RAJVI TRIVEDI

Contents

Foreword

Foreword

Chakrapani Estarla, Principal, Silver Bells Public School

Rajvi Trivedi completed her schooling at Silver bells public school, Bhavnagar. She started her journey with the school and I have seen her grow up. Being the Principal of the school, I have seen Rajvi's work, her growth and her potential. She was always creatively oriented, she would actively participate in various events, and she was especially interested in dancing. She would never miss a chance to perform at the school. Whether it is a festival or the school annual day, we will always see Rajvi perform. Rajvi has also performed on national and international platforms with school team.

Rajvi was a bright student, and she had a good academic record. Though her major interest during school time was dancing, she still managed to balance both dance and academics. I taught her political science and sociology in Grade 11th and 12th. I observed her interest in humanities and I believed that she had the potential to excel. I also enjoyed teaching her.

Rajvi stood out because she was firm and clear about what she wanted to do. She was awarded the Best student Award and best dancer award in the academic year 2015-16 when she completed her schooling. I wish her the all the very best for all her future endeavours.

Principal
Chakrapani Estarla
07 November 2024

Shantinagar, Kalvibid, Bhavnagar 364 002. Ph. : (0278) 2566711, 2569250
E-mail : enquiries@silverbellspublicschool.org ● Website : www.silverbellspublicschool.org

Foreword - Students

Ciya Alex

I would always have hundreds of things to say about my best teacher, Rajvi Ma'am. I have great pride in being one of her students and she has had a great impact on me as a teacher today. She was my Social Sciences pedagogy facilitator in my teacher training college.

The teachers we fondly remember are usually the ones who cared, was passionate, inspired us, observed the best potential in us, provided thoughtful platforms, motivated and shined the guiding light to self-discovery, that's who Rajvi Ma'am is to me. Similarly, as a teacher today, I experience the impact she had on me as I listen, observe and create spaces for my students to discover, learn and grow into the best versions of themselves.

She to me has been that one different essence that inspires my sense of being a teacher. Be it online or offline, she knows the art of keeping the class engaged and memorable as she dedicatedly pours her heart, mind and soul into planning and executing each class.

When I think back about those days, I remember how she would make an effort to know each of her students' strengths by devoting the last few minutes of her class to give space for us to showcase our talents. This knowledge about her students would then be integrated into her lessons seamlessly. She would always guide her students towards opportunities that suited and showcased their specific strengths. She had been a friend and a mentor by observing, listening and understanding our potential. She would then carefully and mindfully create spaces and opportunities for us. Personally, she recognized my interest in performance art and encouraged me to perform a monologue for Women's day. This provided me with the conviction to believe in myself and my own capabilities during a time I was questioning my own capabilities. There have been many instances where her former students have been grateful for her guidance. Many times teachers are too critical without being constructive. What I have observed was that those who were shy would take a chance in that positive environment created by her. This would reflect in their dedication to perform better in life's challenges. This inspires them to be the teacher they needed when they were young and impressionable.

I have also been fortunate to attend her global citizenship events where we had different groups of people coming together to discuss pressing issues such as sustainability and women empowerment through analysing documentaries, developing new ideas to implement in our teaching philosophy through reviewing movies such as Dead Poets Society.

The challenges and opportunities of teaching in the 21st century are unlike anything we've encountered before. From the rise of digital technologies to the shift in pedagogical paradigms, we are living through a revolution that reshapes how education is delivered and experienced.

This book explores these changes with a thoughtful eye, examining the role of technology, inclusivity, and learner-centred approaches in reshaping education. It is not just a guide to adapting to these changes but an invitation to be part of a broader movement—one that demands educators to rethink traditional boundaries, question old models, and courageously experiment with new ones.

In your hands, you hold not just a compilation of ideas and strategies, but a vision for the future of education—one where the needs of every learner, no matter their background or circumstance, are met with creativity, compassion, and purpose. This book will serve as both a compass and a source of inspiration as you continue to shape the minds of tomorrow's leaders, thinkers, and innovators. This is going to be a modern, much required outlook to the vision she has as a passionate and successful educator. It presents to you the struggle between mainstream mentality and inner voice trying to break free.

Asha Kumari

I first met Rajvi as a student in a large batch of 100. Having joined the course late, I felt overwhelmed and lost amid the sea of faces. My first uplifting experience came when Rajvi reached out with personal feedback on an assignment I had submitted. At that moment, I truly felt seen for the first time. What amazed me even more was her ability to make all 100 of us feel acknowledged and valued. In today's highly commercialised educational environment, where the focus is often on developing technical skills, encountering someone who reignites your passion for the profession is a rare gift. For me, Rajvi embodies that gift. As our relationship has evolved from that of a student-teacher to being friends, I eagerly anticipate watching her growth as an educator, artist, and change-maker.

Her classes stood out for the way she was attuned to the needs of the students and the way she approached the most mundane topics. She actively showed us how to use dramatisation and role play to make the classes more engaging; how to keep students in the centre and encourage critical thinking in them through active discussions and creating a safe space to have such healthy discussions without the fear of being judged or labelled.

This book would be a treasure trove for all aspiring educators as well as those who feel stuck in the never ending rat race to get in touch with their true selves and find their way back to their true passion.

Note From The Writer

Thank you for picking up this book. I would like to tell you that I am not a writer. There is no rocket science in this book. I hold no expertise in writing, and you are free to spot some errors, grammatically or otherwise. This book is just an honest record of my journey. I have written this book because I wanted to share some of the important instances of my life with everyone. I felt that this story might help someone.

I also must mention that I do not intend to hurt anyone's sentiments or any ideologies. I do not intend to defame any institution. I do not intend to promote dropping out courses. I do not mean to misrepresent anything. I only put forth certain important instances and questions. In all possible ways, this book is just to bring people's attention to important questions about education. I urge educators, mentors and leaders to look into some of these questions.

I also must say that I did not put myself on any pedestal while I wrote this book. I don't dismiss any other thought or perspective. I am only encouraging a dialogue through this book about certain issues that we observe around. Please read this book with an open mind and feel free to share your feedback with me.

Acknowledgements

I am thankful to a lot of people, because without their support I would not have written this book. First and Foremost, I thank my parents for their constant support in all my endeavours. My parents taught me to dream, and they also gave me the confidence to fulfil those dreams.

I also thank my partner who was always by my side through the ups and downs. He encouraged me to complete this book and he always appreciated all my efforts.

I would like to thank the Principal of my school for the foreword and for teaching me. I am grateful to all my teachers and Guru for everything they taught me. I have learnt a lot and I feel inspired to do better because of them.

I would like to thank all my students. My students are the ones who always make me feel happy. They are the ones who helped me believe in myself. I owe a lot to my students. I would like to thank Ciya Alex and Asha Kumari for writing the foreword and Radhika Mookerjee for designing the meaningful illustrations of this book.

I also thank Kanchi Pandya and Chintan Pandya for helping me with some beautiful ideas for the title and cover page of this book. They have always supported me in my creative endeavours and I am grateful. I would like to extend my gratitude to Anuj Khandelwal who helped design the cover page and who has also contributed a lot to the success of Sattva- A Space for Lifelong Learning.

I thank Notion press for the smooth publication process and all their support.

Lastly, I thank everyone who has helped me find my potential and who has appreciated my work. You all have added a lot of value to my journey.

The Little Aspiring Change Maker

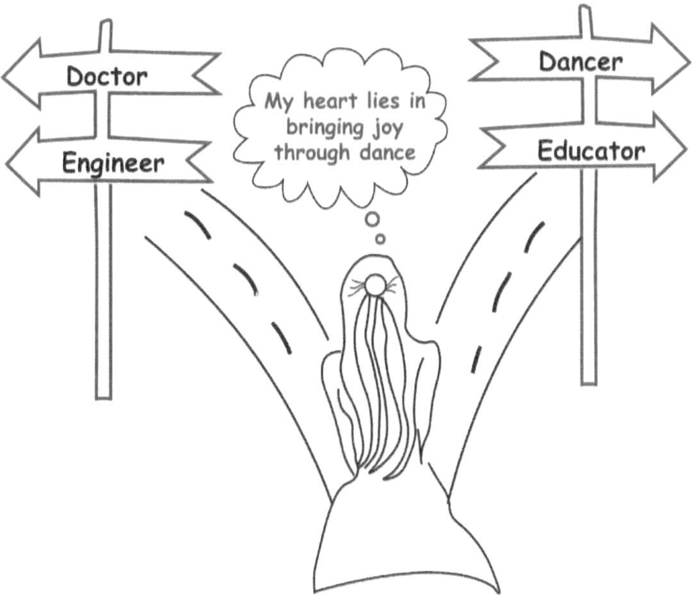

"If you don't allow me to opt for humanities, I won't have any other alternative but to leave this school and find another way", I informed the principal of my school. If one had a look at my report cards, I would definitely be considered as a child having an excellent academic record, eligible to opt for science and commerce streams. Unfortunately, these report cards are not meant for assessing the person in a holistic manner. They can only define how well I performed in my examinations and assignments. An honest assessment would rather show that I was more creative and artistically driven. We live in a society where we follow a hierarchy of disciplines wherein Science remains at the top, and humanities at the bottom. We live in a society where we have set criteria for defining who falls in the category of bright students. Now, these so-called bright students must pursue these highly prestigious and highly paying careers including being a Doctor, an Engineer or a Chartered Accountant. Our perspective on education is also quite materially oriented wherein we think that investing in education must result in great returns- a highly paying job. Similarly, I was also told by people around, by school authorities and others that I had the potential to take up science or commerce for 11th and 12th grade, pursue one of these highly paying careers and thus, follow the herd. But, I was clear about what I wanted to pursue.

Martha Nussbaum (2010) affirms, *"The real clash of civilisation is a clash within the individual, as greed and narcissism contend against respect and love, all modern societies are losing the battle. If we do not insist on the critical importance of the humanities and arts, they will drop away because they do not make money."* We are so distracted by the idea of gaining wealth, that we are solely focusing on churning out job-seekers and profit makers rather than thoughtful citizens. Humanities are not valued. It is seen as a stream meant for those who score poor in their exams, and who have no potential to do well. We don't recognise that the world can benefit so much with humanities and liberal arts education. We need to turn to humanities if we want to develop essential skills like critical thinking, creativity and if we want to build thoughtful global citizens.

I was always told that I had the potential to do well in any field I chose to go to, but I was invariably connected with arts and the social sciences. I had the innate urge to be creative, to find my own ways and to change things around from the initial years of my life. Thankfully, I had the opportunity to learn to dance, to learn Kathak and through dancing find a way of channelising my energy and expressing myself. Along with being a performer, I had also dreamt of being a teacher. Inspired by a lot of my teachers, I felt that I could also create an impact through my classes. I used to enjoy those sessions when I got a chance to present something to the class and I would always try to make it interesting for everyone. This passion for dancing, and the idea of creating impact through education had encouraged me to study humanities. Apart from this, I knew that I had absolutely no interest in Sciences or Mathematics. Now that I am writing this book, I can admit that I hardly attended Maths and physics classes in my 10th grade. I was waiting to get done with these subjects forever. Despite being the only student, my school gave me an opportunity to study humanities for 11th and 12th grade. This marked the beginning of my journey as an aspiring changemaker, as someone who wanted to experiment, who refused to follow the herd, who wanted to break free and who wanted to follow her heart.

Like any other child, I had my orientation towards certain subjects. I would enjoy language classes, social sciences classes and run away from the Maths and Science classes. I still remember how I managed to pass without attempting a single question from the physics section in my boards examination. While many disciplinarians would look down upon this, I can happily reveal that running away to the dance room was much better than sitting in a Mathematics class, pretending to solve a question I did not understand at all. Not that I am promoting bunking classes, but I must say that not all children are born to become doctors and engineers. Some of them will become artists, some will go into sports, and some will probably start an enterprise of their own. They will eventually grow and find their paths. But, we, the society and the systems fail to understand this basic idea. We want all children to be rankers, toppers, smart people and successful in a very rudimentary sense. We need to allow children to just be themselves, make their own set of mistakes and carve their paths. I often ask this question, why are we so obsessed with producing photocopies of students? Why do we want all of them to be the same in every sense? Why can't we allow for diversity? Why do we fail to notice the different abilities and talents children are born with? It is only when I started pursuing my degree in education that I realised that my questions were not irrelevant. And it is not just the career paths that we define for children, but we also define the desirable personality traits and the behaviour of "the ideal child". Even outside the classroom, we have a lot of labels and comments for how children should be.

I always wanted to pursue dancing, and become an artist. Apart from my parents and a few loved ones, every other sane adult considered this path of being an artist as futile. They all came and told me to look out for something else. I was advised to become anything else but an artist. My art had no value, if I can't get all As in my report card. If I manage to get all As, I am an all rounder otherwise, a failure. Art is good for a hobby, it is meant to be an "extracurricular activity". This is how we look at art. For all those who think that children learn important things only in the classroom, and that pursuing arts for career is a big no, I would like to clarify what all Kathak has taught me. It is this hobby through which I was able to survive, thrive and also make a living. It is this art form that empowered me, and that gave me the most rewarding experiences of life. I kept pursuing dancing and Kathak throughout and it has played a beautiful role in my journey. I love being called a performing artist as much as an educator.

This art form has helped me gain confidence, it has helped me feel worthy and validated during some of the most difficult phases of my life. Kathak and my guru helped me understand the value of being humble and grounded. I learnt from Murliben Meghani, a disciple of the Great Guru Pandit Shri Birju Maharaj. Later I also got opportunities to learn from the Guru himself and Vidushi Saswati Sen. She inspired me a lot. She was and continues to be my role model. The art form helped me communicate and express better. More than anything else, it helped me reflect, find my creative urge and gave me a perspective. These are skills that most schools in the present context fail to develop. I won't say that my education did not play any role in my growth, but I have gained invaluable lessons and support from dancing all my life. It is this cultural heritage that we feel proud about, this heritage that is valued and appreciated so much outside of India, and it is this very heritage that we also want to keep our kids away from. Strange, isn't it?

I was always a quiet child, one who enjoyed being alone, and being on my own. I would open up only with a few people. I couldn't deal with too many people, crowded spaces and noise. Clearly, I would enjoy playing with a doll, reading or being alone rather than talking to friends or going out with them. But almost everyone made me feel that something was seriously wrong about it. Many came and told my parents to have another child so that I could turn into a people's person. Let me tell you this approach doesn't work. I can give you examples of extroverts who did not have siblings. I am extremely happy and grateful that I am an only child, and so are my parents. Teachers would tell my parents that I need to speak more in the class. I knew things, I did not have to say those things out loud to show that I knew. I fail to understand why it is so wrong to be quiet, to enjoy silence and peace and to not necessarily need company. If people like being on their own, it is absolutely fine. Please let them be. They are not abnormal. I was often asked these questions. How will you appear in an interview? How will you teach if you remain so quiet? How will you establish yourself in this world if you don't talk? These questions used to make me feel anxious. I was a career oriented person and I wanted to do everything to be good enough for my career. Insecurities would often haunt me. But this does not mean that I must change my personality and start speaking. Why do we believe that only the one who talks, is the one who knows things? Susan Cain (2012) in her book Quiet, writes,*"There's zero correlation between being the best talker and having the best ideas."* Why do we assume that people who are quiet are dumb and can't do much? Another quote from the book Quiet by Susan Cain (2012) affirms, *"Or at school you might have been prodded to come "out of your shell"—that noxious expression which fails to appreciate that some animals naturally carry shelter everywhere they go, and that some humans are just the same."* I couldn't help but relate to how apt this book is for introverts finding their ways in a world that can't stop talking.

We want children to be smart. When we say smart, it can mean a lot of things. We want them to be smartly dressed, we want them to have linguistic fluency, we want them to be quick at crossing roads, we want them to be adventurous, we want them to be super energetic always and we want them to fit into the definition of a normal child. Any uncommon trait is just unacceptable. We want children to be scoring well, but we also label them as being nerdy and boring. How do we define a smart child? How do we define a normal child? And moreover, should we even define or label? How easily do we label children as fat, thin, too shy, too quiet, dull, smart, bright and so on... we have no clue about the impact it creates on the child and how long this stays with the child. I used to be a chubby kid and I was always told that I was fat. I was made fun of because I looked a certain way. It is still a part of me. Today when I create content for my social media pages, this strikes me. Instead of focusing on the content, I end up analysing my appearance all the time. Even when I was not fat, I couldn't get that thought out of my head. I could never see my pictures and videos without thinking about those comments regarding me being fat, chubby, and so on. I firmly believe that it is one's art that adds beauty and not one's appearance, but it is this one principle that I can't stand by in practice.

I have always been conscious about my appearance. Even after I left home and went to other cities, I was preoccupied with these thoughts. However well I did in life, I was always scared of going back home because there would be a set of people ready to comment on my appearance. They will not greet me, they will first comment on whether I gained weight or lost weight. I felt like I had to lose some weight before I went home. How I wish people recognised and appreciated efforts and work more than appearance. Whether school or social circles, how aware are we? Are we sensitising our kids to be kind to others? We label them really quick and they learn labelling at such an early age. We are always ready to judge the book by its cover page. Wouldn't it be better if we just met people without being so keenly observant about their looks?

This discourse brings me to some important questions: What are the attributes that we want our children to acquire? Do we want our children to be insensitive so they could laugh when someone falls down or do we want them to be compassionate such that they take action to help others? Do we want our children to carry on this attitude of "I don't bother if it doesn't affect me" or do we want them to be responsible citizens? Should we teach children to constantly compete with others or should we teach them to learn from one another and grow together? What is it that we want to pass on to the next generation? All these questions need serious reflection. Before we label, before we comment and say that a child is not normal, we need to rethink.

It was difficult for me to strike a balance between the mainstream mentality and my inner voice. I have followed my inner voice always and

I am happy that I did so. I tried my best to not succumb to the pressure of fitting in. Robert Frost (1970) said, *"Two roads diverged in a wood, and I—I took the one less travelled by and that has made all the difference."* I absolutely love this quote. It gives the right words to my feelings. I wanted to be this person who does something pathbreaking. It was not about becoming popular. It was about doing things that mattered. It was about following the inner voice and passion. And that is exactly what happened when my school recognized the efforts of a humanities student, and opened up the alternative for humanities for students. There were around 15 to 20 students who joined.

This doesn't mean that I was always right. I am not boasting that my thoughts were the only valid ones and I am not even dismissing any other thought. I am not trying to impose anything as the ultimate truth. I am only sharing my thoughts and my questions. In fact, I am urging you to look at multiple perspectives, to look at the impact of comments and labelling, and to look at how children grow up and they hold things close to their hearts (good and bad). I had different thought processes, I had anger issues at times and I made many mistakes like any other child would. But I was allowed to be myself and grow at my pace and that happened because my parents created that kind of an atmosphere for me.

CHAPTER II

The ABC's of Good Parenting

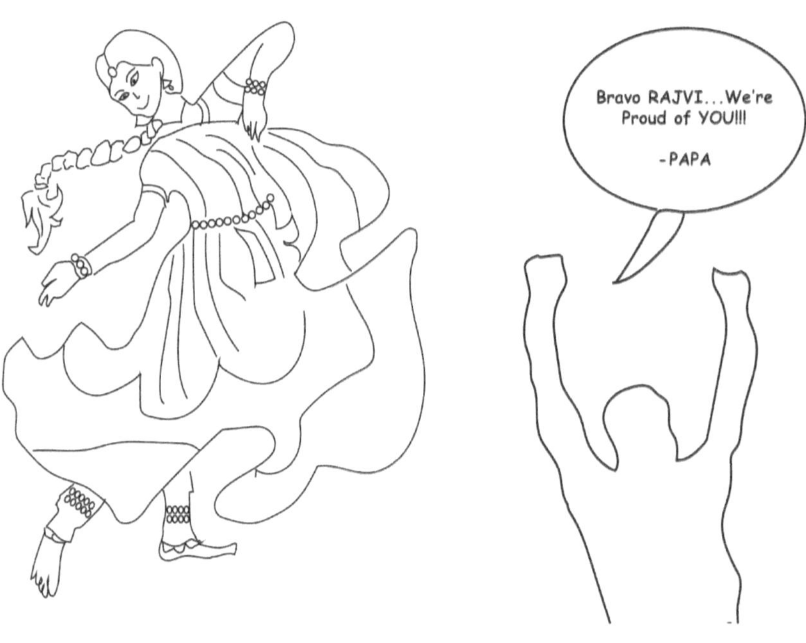

"Gun guna rahe hai bhavre, khil rahi hai kali kali", an old hindi song plays on the television, my father calls me, and says see your favourite song is up. I come running with a cheerful smile on my face. It was not just the song that was the reason for my smile, but also the time of the day. It was around 9 PM, the time when we would sit together and listen to some old songs, and then go out for a small ride. I enjoy listening to some of these old songs and ghazals with my parents. I rejoice in spending time with my parents, whether listening to songs, watching movies or going out for trips. If I was accompanied by my parents, I would ask for nothing else.

As the usual mindset goes, parents are considered to be rather strict, or the ones who are ever ready to give lectures "gyaan" in popular terms these days, and the ones who would impose rules and regulations in the house. But, this wasn't my case. My parents are more fun-loving than I am, they are young at heart and full of life. They were always my best friends, and they continue to be. In fact, people usually go on a Goa trip with their friends, but I have been on one with my parents, and what a luxury it was!

Parenting is usually ridden with expectations. At times, even before children are born, their parents have a full-fledged plan prepared for them. What path will they walk on, what career will be best suited for them, what traditions will they carry forward, and what dreams and goals will fuel their lives- everything is planned and predetermined. In such cases, is there any room for children to explore, find their ways, and make their set of mistakes? Is there any room for children to turn into adults who can think for themselves and make good decisions? Is there any scope for blossoming of children into happy individuals? At times, these expectations are so high, so harsh that children lose track of everything and live their entire lives feeling pressurised. We all have heard of cases wherein children commit suicides, or run away or take to undesired habits/paths because of such pressure. While we are happy to observe a few changes around these days, we also see pregnant ladies (to-be-mothers) attending some maths classes so that the child is born a genius and can successfully clear the JEE-NEET examinations. Of course the full-fledged plan contains only a few career options including being a doctor, engineer or a C.A. Not many parents think of having kids so that they can some day get a gold medal in olympics. The majority of parents would certainly tell their children to focus on studies, and not on sports, dance, music, art, etc. For me, apart from eating right (FYI, I was a really picky eater and loved junk) and enjoying myself, my parents never had any expectations. I was free to choose my path.

My parents have always stood by my side with love and pride. They have always encouraged me to give my best shot in whatever I chose to do. They have provided tremendous support in my journey of being a performing artist. When I was a kid, I would dream of performing in those reality shows. Little did I know that my journey was not about contesting with others on a television screen, it was something else. Still, my parents would take me to different cities and places for auditions. They wanted me to experience everything and then decide for myself what works best. Not that my parents let me live in a dreamy world, where I was never exposed to reality. My mother always pushed me to improve. She appreciated me, but she also pointed out if there was any scope for improvement. There were times when I felt disappointed. I felt like why would she not be satisfied with my work ever. But, only later, I realised that she wanted me to do the best. She is undoubtedly the reason for my growth. Though they told me that I needed to improve, they always believed in my potential and they said it out loud to me. This is a thought for parents out there. Yes, you must tell your children to do better, but you must also tell them that they are doing good, you must also appreciate them and show them that you are there if something goes wrong.

While learning Kathak, I also received wonderful opportunities to learn from the Great Guru- Pandit Shri Birju Maharajji and Vidushi Saswati Sen. We have not missed a single workshop. My parents took me to different cities, Ahmedabad, Mumbai and everywhere else. They did everything possible for my growth, my happiness. Not once did my parents say that dancing won't help you make money, you should probably do something more substantial for your career. I remember I was in 12th grade and when I first heard about the opportunity to perform in Russia, I had no intention of going. I shared with my parents about this event and mentioned that this is only a partially funded trip and I don't think I can do this. My parents, and even my grandparents jumped into the conversation and said, yes you are definitely going. They did not even think about the finances and they just wanted me to make the best of all opportunities. This support, and confidence is what keeps me going even today and I must say I feel blessed to have been born to my parents.

It is in this discussion that I want to put forth a very important question for parents. Do you want your children to be afraid of you or do you want them to respect you? Do you want to be seen as perfect aliens or as humans who make mistakes, have their own set of struggles, and can connect well? What is the kind of atmosphere you want to create for your children? I often come across parents who present themselves as these flawless, "know-it-all" kind of people, and they believe that children must be kept under control, and that fear is the only tool to discipline them. I know about parents beating their children for petty issues, and even encouraging teachers to beat their children at school if they don't "behave". These are the same parents who then complain about their children being distant from them, and not willing to spend time with them. I know that I am not a parent, and hence you might feel like questioning my perspective here. However, I have been a teacher and from my understanding and experience, I can firmly state that fear as a tool to discipline is irrelevant today.

I believe that it is important for all of us to understand that we are all humans, and we are not perfect beings. Especially as parents, rather than creating a facade about perfection, people should normalise being themselves in front of their children. I saw my parents as normal humans who had their own set of struggles, dreams, and stories. They appeared as people who make mistakes, who learn, who evolve and who are approachable. And this is exactly why I also got to make my own set of mistakes and a space to be myself, explore and grow. I was not afraid of my parents, for I knew they wouldn't hit me, or shout at me. But I respected them and I never wanted to disappoint them. My parents came from a background where they never encouraged hitting children, or using violence or force as a means to discipline. I still remember, once a teacher slapped a child in my class and it was very disturbing for me. The next day, my mom was at school and she made it clear that such instances can create a negative impact on children's minds and thus should be avoided.

I wouldn't say that it was all sweet and cheesy all the time with my parents. I don't say that I lived in some utopian kind of a space. In fact, it was always very real. There were times when my parents would get upset because of my behaviour, or they wanted me to take things seriously and I would have been reluctant. There have been times when mom would be angry with me, and my father would come as a saviour. But, it never happened that I felt distant from my parents, or I felt like I didn't belong here. At times I was wrong, at times they were wrong, but we accepted that and moved forward. Whatever it was, I always wanted to come back to my parents for everything. My parents made sure that they were by my side, whatever the situation might be. And that is why even when I failed miserably, they did not stop believing in me. They stood by me and always pushed me to dream big and keep working towards my goals. I feel that I have become a better individual at many levels because of the kind of nurturing I have received, the kind of love and support I have received from my parents.

Often when we talk about strict parents, we have a tendency to say that parents have had a tough time in the past and their circumstances have made them who they are. People feel that parents might pass on their generational trauma to their children in various ways and that is okay. But, who stops this cycle then? If we do not reflect upon our actions and keep following something that is outdated or irrelevant, then how is it possible to change anything for the better? I can with pride say that my parents also have had their struggles, they have had tough times, and some unfulfilled dreams, but those were never imposed on me. They did not pass on their trauma to the next generation, they chose to give me a better life instead. In fact, they wanted me to never deal with problems that they had to deal with.

One of the most beautiful things my parents helped me learn was the value of simplicity. My parents provided for everything that was necessary for me. They also managed to instil within me this love for simplicity. I like owning minimal, I believe in the ideology of less is more, and I am a calculative person. My parents have always given me more than what was needed and that is why I never craved for more-more attention, or more resources. I was blessed with so much at home that I never felt the need to seek something outside of home. Rather than encouraging me to be a part of the race and earn money, they always pushed me to follow my passion and pursue happiness. Even now, when I feel tense or anxious about something, my parents are my go to. They have developed some wonderful values including gratitude, simplicity and more and this has supported me in becoming a better person.

My parents are blessed with beautiful connections and I got the fruits of the same. I was raised in a culture that was safe, happy and supportive. I must mention Madhuvan here. Madhuvan is a second home for me, whatever I achieve I have to share it with people at Madhuvan. My family at Madhuvan has always inspired me and I am grateful for the same. I value these relations more than any blood relations. These relations there is so much reciprocity, support and freedom that one cannot ask for me. Because of these connections, I developed this love for art. I was raised in a wonderful environment and that has shaped me into a better human being. My family, my parents and these relationships portray the idea that family promotes freedom. One's family should not be a space where one feels restricted and bound by rules and traditions, family should be a space where one feels like one is free, one will always have the support of family even in the worst of the times.

I must also mention that I was born in a context when male-child preference was highly prevalent. People desired sons more than daughters, and they thought that ultimately girls have to be married. We get to observe such orthodox mentality even today, but back then it was more overtly visible. Today we are surrounded by people who call themselves "progressive" but still believe that investing in gold is the best thing one can do for one's daughters. I have been a witness to parents who would pressurise their daughters to get married, and who would not even think about their growth. On the contrary, my parents never thought about my marriage; they always told me to carve my own path, and motivated me to have an identity of my own. In a world where women are unsafe, and where women have to work twice as much as men to prove their worth, I am blessed with parents who are so progressive and supportive. My parents never made me feel that marriage is the ultimate goal of my life. They wanted me to reach new heights with a partner, or without one. They would often tell me to go around the world, travel, explore and do whatever makes me happy. We are not here to follow any timelines.

Our society constantly tells women to get married, have kids and settle down. We live in a society wherein women still have to struggle and fight for their rights, for their dreams. I have seen both men and women around me suffering because of patriarchy, and I used to feel passionately about the same. I have fought aggressively for women, and people know that this gender inequality is something that continues to bother me. It angers me to note that even in this "modern" era, in this 21st century, women cannot make decisions for themselves. Women are judged for their dressing choices, their career choices, their personal choices (getting married, deciding not to have kids), and their cooking skills, of course. Don't you think it is high time that we reflect on what kind of culture we want to create? It is time to end these debates and treat both men and women like humans. Is it so difficult?

I can say with pride that my parents never invested in gold, they rather thought of investing in my talent, my potential. They did not dream of having a big fat wedding for me, but they did dream about doing a big stage performance in the city. As far as I remember, I always wanted to have a simple court marriage, and make the least possible noise. Other parents might argue that we need to go according to the norms of the society. My parents supported me in my decisions and were also ready to fight for me. A popular question that parents ask children is "what will others say?", but this was never the case for me. My parents would have dealt with those "others" very politely. When daughters have such support from their parents, they can do wonders and I urge you all to raise your daughters with utmost love and support so that they can grow up and stand tall on their feet. My parents, and especially my nana (maternal grandfather) always said this one thing- "Rajvi, Sky's the limit. Dream big". This thought keeps me alive even today, it uplifts me every time I feel low or disheartened.

Parents don't necessarily have to be strict and perfect beings, they just have to be approachable humans, and that is all a child can ask for. I will reiterate that I understand I am not a parent, and I might not know all the aspects around parenting. But I am someone who has experienced the fruits of good parenting and it is through this perspective that I have written this entire chapter.

"Your children are not your children.

They are the sons and daughters of Life's longing for itself.

They come through you but not from you,

And though they are with you yet they belong not to you."

Khalil Gibran, The Prophet (Knopf, 1923).

CHAPTER III

Gold Medals, Are They Enough?

A new set of questions had emerged before me now. I had to select a city, a university and a course for my Bachelors degree. I was a little confused initially about what to do, and I did not have everything figured out. Students are usually expected to know everything, have everything figured out. Society judges you the minute you say that you don't know enough and you are still exploring the available courses and degrees. To all students out there, please remember that it is absolutely okay to not know everything and it is normal to feel a little confused. You can have questions, you can change your career path a little later, and you can jump into something completely different from what was planned. Feel free to experiment, make some decisions and enjoy the process of growing. I am not trying to sound like some saintly personality, but honestly no one has everything figured out. Not even that uncle who told you to focus and make the right decisions always. If one is willing to be a learner, half of the things are sorted. One eventually finds the right direction if one is fueled by passion.

I was experiencing mixed feelings, anxious because I had to leave home, stay away from my parents, and excited because going to college and adulting was something I always dreamt of. The bollywood films had played a huge role in shaping my perceptions about universities, and I must admit that these perceptions were quite unreal. As an artist, I was waiting to be a part of all co-curricular activities and youth festivals. I had heard stories from my mother about her youth festivals and how she travelled across the country and performed on various platforms. And here was my opportunity to perform and present my creativity to the world. I was really excited, I wanted to attend all classes, participate in all events and make the most of my college life.

To my surprise I picked a city that was never on my list and a university for which we received all mixed reviews. To be honest, these were last minute changes in my plans. I selected those because I wanted to study sociology. Even today, I like calling myself a sociology student because it has played a pivotal role in moulding my beliefs, ideas and also personality to an extent. Later my path changed, but I still like studying sociology. This subject gives me a sense of validation that my thoughts, my questions about society are valid. I can have a strong set of opinions, and most importantly I can be a changemaker. I can be sensitive to the issues around me and I don't have to be a bystander and do nothing about what is wrong or unjust. People always say that one cannot change things around, one must ignore the evils of the society and move on. Thankfully, Sociology saved me. Sociology allowed me to express myself better and also made me realise that whatever I become, I want a career through which I can make this society a better place to live in. My role models were not the richest people, but those who were great speakers, great teachers and great change makers. I always wanted to be financially independent, but money wasn't the only aim that pushed me, I wanted to work for a more rewarding experience.

On one hand, there were some wonderful experiences and lessons learnt while I pursued my B.A. in Sociology and M.A. in Education. The subject I selected for Masters was rather unpopular. There were not many students who selected this program. But when I studied sociology, I realised the fundamental role of education in changing mindsets, in transforming societies. If you have noticed, discussions about any social issue would usually translate to one basic solution- Quality Education. For me it was impossible to think of society without education and vice-versa. My personal experiences also encouraged me to study Education as a discipline. I tried giving my best in every activity, every event. I did my projects on time, and with dedication. I looked forward to some of my creative assignments. I did not skip any seminar or conference that revolved around subjects of my interest. I made efforts to connect with like-minded people and made some good friends. I led some cultural events and conferences during my masters degree and that helped me feel a little more confident. I also had good relationships with most of my teachers and some of them inspired me a lot. Everyday I dreamt of standing there, where those teachers were standing and taking classes. Though I was always excited about what was happening outside the boundaries of my class, I still sincerely completed my degrees with good grades and met all the expectations. I got opportunities to work in some international exchange programs, and I also cleared NET because by then I had realised how much I enjoyed teaching and that I was also good at building rapport with students and young people.

On the other hand, college life wasn't as dreamy and happening as I thought it would be. It was not easy to step out of that comforting space at home, and march into an unknown terrain. I did not have to struggle for basic necessities, or resources, but I had to face other difficulties. As soon as I stepped out in this new place, I felt extremely pressurised and I started feeling a need for validation. First year in college and my self-image was a big zero. I started to feel a little too competitive, an innate urge to prove my worth. I had to show the world that I could do something, I wasn't just another girl from a small town, but I had the potential to do a lot. I always felt that whatever I was doing was not good enough. I missed my home a little more for this reason, I wanted to be seen, heard, appreciated and loved. At every step, I felt haunted by this one question- What if I don't succeed in ways defined by society?

I was a gold medalist throughout, a scholarship holder for Bachelors and Masters degrees. But even that was not enough to make me feel worthy. In fact I was often told that I might be good at books and exams, but I can't be as good at work. I might not be skilled enough for a job. I might not be able to handle interviews. I was always afraid that what if I don't get a high-paying job? What if I don't get recognized for my work? I kept looking for external factors (people, opportunities) to come and validate my efforts rather than look inside and believe in my potential. When someone appreciated me, I felt boosted and empowered. However, this shouldn't be the case. Institutions, systems and the entire culture around should not win by making you feel like a slave of the system. I feel that these institutions and systems always make you feel inadequate. We need to hustle and we need to show that we are productive all the time. This feeling stayed with me for quite some time. Even today, I struggle to appreciate myself. I am waiting to hear that inner voice that tells me that I am good enough. Why is it so difficult to accept ourselves? Why can't we accept our mistakes, failures, weaknesses and move on? Why do we consider life a race, and not a journey? Why is it so difficult to believe in our own potential? Do we get a chance to tap into our potential? Do the systems around allow us to feel empowered and perfect the way we are? Questions to consider, right?

I also never really connected with the people and culture. I wasn't smart enough for the world. I had ideas but I never felt the need to make noise about these ideas. I could not fit into a system where the one whose voice is loudest wins the argument. People around me couldn't stop talking, and I never felt a sense of belonging. I was afraid of being a dumb in the crowd that knew how to showcase their knowledge and potential. I often felt alienated. I did not succumb to the pressure of listening to english songs, watching english movies, being active on social media all the time, drinking, smoking, partying and being "cool". My definition of having fun was so different that I always wanted to be left alone. People in college are expected to dress up according to the latest trends and standards and I did not follow those. I dressed based on my comfort zone and my choices. I absolutely love old hindi songs, ghazals and classical music. Rather than partying I would just dance for an hour practising some of my old choreographies, and I loved dressing traditionally. Not that I did these things to stand out, I did not appreciate that people have to be a certain way to fit into the crowd and belong. I enjoyed being on my own and working towards my goals. Not that I never took a day off, or never lazed around or never celebrated. Just that I had my own ways of celebrating. And honestly, should we also define the ways of celebrating? Can we not have some individual choices at least in this case? I liked celebrating and taking a day off, but that would be different from the normal celebration. I don't like the fact that we have to change ourselves to fit into a norm created by others in the society.

Throughout my college life, I wondered what motivates students to attend classes? What brings them to the University? In my Bachelors, the college administration never really paid any attention to the number of students attending classes. We get to see our classmates directly on the day of examination. There were 3 to 5 people who came regularly and paid attention to what was happening in classes. Although there were less facilities, fewer students in class, teachers used to take engaging classes. In my Masters, students had to come to classes because there was a strict rule about having 85 percent of attendance. It was such a strict system that students dragged themselves to class every single day. There were a lot of facilities available including technology, benches, etc. but the teachers came and just read presentations. Only a few teachers were able to engage students. Others were just providing notes. In both these cases, we rarely see students coming to class because they are actually looking forward to learning. It is not for learning or academic rigour, students came to class only because of a rule. So then, are institutions failing to provide experiences that motivate students to attend classes? Are these institutions even relevant in the present context?

As a child and as an adult, I dreamt of participating in youth festivals. These are inter-college festivals that include a variety of events including folk dance, classical dance, elocution, theatre, music, folk orchestra, art, and others. These festivals provide students an opportunity to explore their own potential, connect with others, learn skills like teamwork, creative thinking and provide a safe space to showcase their talent. Post the inter-college festivals, the winning teams get to perform at zonal levels, and then at national level. Earlier, universities provided ample time for students to practise, perform and enjoy these festivals. I was looking forward to these festivals. However, to my disappointment, nowadays the youth festival is just another event that has to be done for a formality. It is just another thing on the checklist, just another thing to be documented for NAAC accreditation. The Universities do not really want to organise these festivals for students' well-being. I have seen teachers who called these festivals useless and said that because of these festivals they have a difficulty managing time and completing syllabus. Even in such a context, Universities from small towns like Bhavnagar are making an attempt to maintain the spirit and essence of these festivals. All students are involved in some or the other event, they are not thinking about attendance, they are enjoying the festival and learning. We tend to think that one should study in these big and well known universities for better career opportunities, but at times these not so widely visible institutions are doing way better.

From what I have experienced during my college life, I also want to ask another important question. How many universities actually emphasise students' well-being? Yes, they have their student welfare offices, they have counsellors for every department, they also observe these mental health days and weeks, they have this whole feedback system and everything in place. But are students happy? Are they learning in a stress-free environment? Are those counsellors listening to students or providing some additional administrative support to their department? Do they even consider students' feedback when they discuss new policies or rules? We studied Weber's model of bureaucracy in our sociology classes and I find this model so relevant in the present education system (Birch, 2022). The leadership is far from what is happening on the field, the teachers are busy with administrative work, schools have become mere factories and students feel a sense of disconnection. Universities have become bureaucratic to an extent that if a teacher wants to take a class outside in a different space than their regular classroom, the teacher has to take signatures from ten people asking for their permission to do so. It is this bureaucratic and hierarchical organisational culture of universities that motivated me to study the idea of student alienation. Students feel alienated (isolated) from the process of learning, and they do not have a sense of belonging to their institution, and this affects their overall well-being, their performance as well. This feeling can be different in different institutions, my observations are based on my experiences and the study I conducted during my post-graduation. You might want to argue with me, saying if I was so bright, I should have gone and studied at IITs and some of the other best institutions. Let me break this myth here. They are not doing such a wonderful job in promoting students' well-being. We keep reading about the suicide cases at IITs (Kumar, 2024). You are free to have a look at the references.

But then it is just a degree, get it done with, get a job and move on, right? Why bother asking questions that colleges are not obligated to respond to?

CHAPTER IV

From Learners To Global Citizens- A Long Way To Go!

What is the impact of education on society? Does education help in building citizens who can act for a more sustainable future? The outcomes of learning involve a change in behaviour. I always wondered how we see so many people attending schools, and colleges, getting their degrees and jobs, but we don't necessarily see a change in mindsets and behaviours. An engineer by profession, but still can't follow traffic rules. A Chartered accountant, but still promotes gender inequalities. An IAS officer, but can't stand up against issues like dowry. Literacy rates have improved tremendously since our country got independence, but we have still not completely dealt with issues like dowry deaths, child marriage, rape, superstitions, honour killings and many others.

"In terms of ecological and humanitarian values, both educational researchers and economists have long lamented that there is no correlation between high educational performance and environmentally and socially sustainable actions and behaviours" (Orr, 2004, Sterling, 2010; Phillips, 2020). I think this resonates a lot with the system that we are in right now. We don't send our children to schools, and colleges so that they grow up to become citizens and change makers. We send them so that they can be toppers, they can get into prestigious institutions probably in some foreign country and then get a high paying job. India is blessed with a demographic dividend, meaning the country has a majority of young population. Unfortunately, we want these young people to shrug their shoulders, ignore the issues around and move on with their lives. We don't want them to be citizens, leaders of the future. We don't give these young people a chance to channelise their energy, their capacities in the desired directions. We have successfully inculcated the belief among youngsters that they must ignore what is happening around, they must keep their passion aside and that they cannot change people's mindsets or systems functioning currently.

We all relate with these ideas. Whenever there is a discussion about the education system, we all have a hundred things to share. We all have an opinion about the future of education, and we don't need to be supported by research for this. We understand that education is crucial for the progress of a nation, and we all wish to see some improvement in ways things are working right now. Despite having these opinions, how many of us initiate something to deal with issues around? Take a simple case of cleanliness in your neighbourhood. You will find only a few of them actually doing something about it. We have a lot of policies and literature about how education ideally should be, but how much of this gets translated into practice? We have a lot written on paper, but do we care to take a look at what is happening in our everyday lives. We read the newspapers everyday, we are aware about the injustices, we know a lot, yet we do not want to take any action. Freire (2001) points out that the ultimate goals of education are emancipation and liberation from all injustices (Byker, 2016). I cannot help but agree with Freire, but what happens in reality is far from this thought. Education actually reproduces the status quo and is completely disconnected from the real world.

With these thoughts in mind, I jumped into research. This is what motivated me to pursue PhD in Global Citizenship Education. The existing global challenges, including climate change, exhaustion of resources, disintegrating democracy, injustice, and inequalities urge individuals to work collectively. Educational institutions must take the initiative to address these challenges (Magro, 2015). These daunting global challenges are leading people to reconsider the role of higher education in preparing students for a sustainable future (LaMachia, 2016). Higher education curriculum must reflect the changes occurring in the society and also address the challenges of the society by preparing students for the same. Global citizenship education, as per my research statement, was the response to a lot of evils of the current system. It implies an overall improvement in quality of education, it implies a shift in pedagogy, it implies going beyond the syllabus and bringing the world to the classroom, and it also implies providing a safe and peaceful classroom culture for learning.

I wanted to study the measures taken by universities to promote global citizenship and sustainability. I wanted to examine the gap between what is written in the curricula documents and what is observed in outcomes, student behaviours. I wanted to assess if students are acquiring skills, knowledge and attitudes that can help them become global citizens and can help them thrive in the 21st century.

When I selected this topic, I knew I was stepping into something completely new and untapped. One couldn't find a lot of research on this topic, especially in the Indian context. This did not scare me, it in fact gave me a boost. I always wanted to work on something that was less explored, and do my research in a way that I can add some value to the existing research. It wasn't easy, because even the faculty members were not well-versed with the idea. Since this was new, I was hopeful that I would be able to make a good contribution and hence, I was looking forward to my research. I also received a lot of support from APCEIU UNESCO, an organisation that is working relentlessly in the field of global citizenship education. They provided a lot of opportunities for me to learn, attend workshops, access reports and materials and connect with some experts in the field.

It was during the first phase of covid that I started doing my PhD. I used to attend online coursework classes in the evenings, and I tried doing some internships alongside. Although online learning was not as effective as in-person, I tried giving my best shot in all classes and assignments. I felt a little lost at times. During the covid phase, all of us went through some ups and downs, and hence it was difficult to be completely focused on PhD. We heard disturbing news from around, we lost many of our loved ones and it was difficult to absorb all of this and yet be completely on track with my research. I had a hundred thoughts about my work, my career and my future continuously running in my mind. But, I was still quite motivated to complete my PhD. I was hopeful that we shall get out of this phase and then things will be sorted again. During this time, I was able to publish some of my research work and that gave me a little confidence that maybe I was on the right track.

These days there is a lot of emphasis on publication, and it is a good thing. It helps enhance the quality of research. But then should everything revolve around publications only? For me, I wanted to make my research available for every other person out there. I wanted to spread the message across to everyone. I used to feel that my research would be meaningless if it doesn't reach students, parents, teachers and other members of society. I did not wish to publish a strong quantitative data based article in a big journal that no one would eventually read. Because of the rules, I tried publishing articles related to my work, but I faced many rejections. Those rejections didn't stop me, because somewhere I knew that this is how my journey is going to be and I was ready to put in more effort. I wanted my research articles to reflect my passion, and not my knowledge of concepts and research methods. I wanted people to start thinking in this direction of transformative learning and global citizenship education.

Pursuing PhD was also a dream I shared with my grandfather. He often encouraged me to do research and teach at universities. I was always encouraged by my family for research. Hence, there were emotions surrounding the PhD. I don't know if this is right or not, but I was always emotional about my work, about my research. I was driven by my emotions, passion and personal experiences. I was unable to detach myself from my PhD, my subject of work. I would often quote some of the readings in my everyday conversations. When we learn something, it is visible in our personalities, our behaviour. As a teacher, one might be working for a fixed set of hours, but that doesn't mean one forgets everything that happened at school the moment one gets back home. Is it wrong to be emotional about your work? Is it not good to be driven by passion and emotion? We see emotions as weakness and we try to hide them. But in reality what is it that is not driven by emotions? The outcome of my research work was going to be my brainchild. I wanted to learn, I wanted to work hard and I wanted to make things work. I wanted to turn that dream into reality. I believe that my emotional connection with my work will take me places and I don't think this is a weakness. I am a sensitive person, my emotions drive me and there is nothing wrong. We focus so much on knowing things, remembering things, that we completely ignore feelings, emotions. People who claim to know a lot are worshipped by society. But people pay least attention to emotions. If we start giving equal importance to emotions, as much as we give to intelligence, we will be able to create a better world. Global Citizenship Education encompasses social-emotional learning and caters to head, heart and hand. The focus is not only on the cognitive abilities (memorising,knowing), but also on holistic development of learners. We need to start prioritising emotions, feelings and attitudes because that is what will help change mindsets.

Working online was difficult. But when we got back to the campus after the initial phases of covid, things changed for good. I got a chance to connect with other PhD scholars and learn about their journeys, their struggles. I enjoyed sitting in the library and working. It was peaceful to just read at times, it was energising to have some engaging coffee conversations with fellow researchers. Research is never easy. It requires a lot of patience, and resilience. You fail a lot, but then you have to bounce back. You face rejections, but you still try and make things work. The entire journey can make you feel exhausted. Talking with friends and fellow researchers was the good part because we realise that all of us are trying, all of us are navigating ways and we can all help each other. I must say I found some really good friends who inspired me by their dedication and commitment to their work. After many ups and downs, many meetings and many changes, I finally got my research proposal approved and this was definitely a moment to celebrate.

In this journey, I was blessed that I had an amazing partner, who not only supported me but also made me feel heard, seen, valued and loved while I was out of my comfort zone. I was a tough nut, but yet I found a friend, a partner who promised to be by my side always. He would often tell me, Rajvi, you are very creative, you have all the potential to do well; you just need to accept yourself and love yourself. Whenever I was frustrated with things around, he would come, meet me and make things right. He was always very patient in dealing with me. Whether it was my dance performance or my research presentation, he was always there to support and cheer for me. It was with this friend, that I could share my joys and sorrows and I could rant continuously about the sick society. Although I never wished or dreamt of having a partner, a loved one, I was grateful to have this sweet one by my side. My journey was going to get even more difficult, and in this journey I feel my partner was definitely godsend.

I received appreciation for my research. I started observing my work more closely. I developed a love for some philosophies, especially those that supported not just my research, but also my worldviews. The path seemed vague at times, I was still determined to complete my research. I saw the dream of presenting my research to the world and I tried working towards that dream. Little did I know what was in store for me...

CHAPTER V

What makes a good teacher?

"The relationship between teacher and pupil can be a vital link through which new horizons are opened and life develops. To me, the essence of education is this process whereby one person's character inspires another. When teachers become partners in the process of discovery, burning with a passion for truth, the desire to learn will naturally be ignited in their students' hearts." - Daisaku Ikeda (2010), Soka Education.

I get a call from my university and the next thing I see - me and my parents getting all emotional. Yes, I was going to teach at the university now. In the call, they mentioned that I will be taking classes for B.Ed students (pre-service teachers). This was something that I had waited for. I had always visualised myself in a saree, with those glasses and few strings of grey hair, and I would enter a classroom full of students. And here was the moment, the beginning of my journey as an educator. I got an opportunity to teach B.Ed students, the future teachers who will create an impact on so many other students. I couldn't have asked for more.

Initially I had to take online classes, and then move on to offline settings. Whether online or offline, I wanted my students to feel heard, seen and valued. I wanted to create a space wherein everyone felt included. From the very first class, I made an attempt to remember my students' names, their interests and their strengths. I encouraged each and every student in my class to participate in the discussion. I tried using some innovative activities such that students who do not like talking also get a chance to share their thoughts, maybe through some written work, mind mapping or art work. There were some rules for my classes. We would welcome every single thought with an open mind. We might disagree with each other, but we would do that with respect. We would engage in discussions in such a way that we allowed everyone to contribute, and we would never bully friends and classmates on the basis of their language, or background or other such factors. This was a safe space, and my students were free to share their opinions. I specifically focused on the culture and environment of the class, because when teachers feel safe and included, they will also make similar efforts in their own future classrooms.

We also agreed to be co-learners in the process, I never wanted to impose myself as an authoritative figure who claimed to be right always, and who cannot be questioned. I wanted to be with them in this journey of learning, by their side and I also sought to learn from them. They definitely knew more than me, I was only there to help them, to facilitate. And this is exactly what teachers need to do in the present context. Gone are the days when we thought that the teacher knows everythings and the students know nothing. With the help of google uncle, these days kids know more than their teachers do. We are here to help them acquire skills, attitudes and we are here so that they can learn higher order thinking. We are here to humanise the process of learning. We are here so that we can pay attention to their different needs and employ diversity for the good of the entire class. Therefore, I made sure to go beyond the textbook, beyond the syllabus and work on skills necessary for 21st century learners.

I believe that the heart of my class has always been the approach, and the pedagogy. I made sure that I speak less, and my students speak more. In this context, where we are dealing with information overload, I tried to give my students the time to absorb things. As teachers we simply walk into a class and start following the plan we have in mind. We often don't give students any time to process everything they are gathering and learning. We had some professors who would ask a question, and give students only 3 seconds to answer. 3 seconds, that too for a social science kind of class. And then begins the race, the one who answers first wins. The other students fail to answer, they will be labelled dumb and useless. Imagine teacher trainers passing this on to future teachers and these future teachers taking this forward to their classrooms. Students might want to add so much, they can bring a lot to the table but do we give them that opportunity? Do we give our students a chance to express themselves?

So for my class, less lecture, more play, more colours and more activity was the thumb rule. We used to have discussions, mind-mapping activities, collaborative activities and a lot more in the class. I would often start my class with a fun exercise so that they get to move a little bit. We all are aware that sitting is the new smoking, but do we even give students a break so that they can get up from their assigned seats and move around, walk around a bit? Even when you work with thirty, forty year old students, you realise that students enjoy working with colours, chart-papers and they enjoy participating in activities at any age. They would feel as excited and curious about the class, as any 4th grade student. One is never too old to have some fun in the class, be curious and learn something new. I don't know if I always succeeded in making my class engaging, but I definitely wanted students to come to the class happily, not just because they needed attendance. It is time that professors start thinking about these questions- What is it that I can do to make my classes fun, engaging and relevant? What motivates students to attend my class?

I loved asking questions. *"A good question can excite, disturb, or comfort, and eventually yield an unexpected bounty of understanding and critical awareness."* (Cline, B. 2024) Questions are the most powerful tools in fueling curiosity and shaping a participative environment in the class. I wanted students to think for themselves, and therefore I made sure I asked some good questions. Questioning is an art that I am still learning. It must be noted that my students also asked a lot of questions. At times, I knew the answer, so I answered. At times, I opened it up for the entire class to discuss. At times, I said I need to do more homework to answer this question. Many teachers find it difficult to accept this, and hence they shut their students down and don't allow students to ask questions. We are humans, we are not computers, we don't have to know everything. We need to stop portraying ourselves as these perfect beings in the class. We can go wrong, we can make a mistake, we might forget something, and that is absolutely fine. Therefore, it is crucial to build a collaborative culture, wherein the teacher and students contribute equally to knowledge construction. We must be careful that we don't paint a child's imagination, we must not impose our ideas and biases, we need to be open to questions, disagreements, and multiple perspectives.

I would often give creative assignments to my students. They can pick up a topic, and create a podcast around the same, or use visual storytelling or do a role play. I wanted to give them an opportunity to select the assignment that they felt they would enjoy the most. In a context where students can use Artificial Intelligence tools and submit a well-written essay without having to think even a bit, I wanted my students to do something of their own, I wanted them to be creative and I always encouraged them to step out of the box. Technology is taking over, and yes students are resorting to these unethical means for their work. However as educators can we not make our assignments fun and engaging so that students want to, and have to do it on their own? Students cheating in their assignments, and resorting to unethical means is one big challenge for sure. In fact, I have been told many times that you can't stop students from cheating. It is not possible. Why? Well the first step here is to practise what we preach. We need to be those models who walk on an ethical path and then expect students to do so. This goes not only for cheating, but for every other aspect. If we shout and scold these future teachers, they will also do the same in their future classrooms. Hence as teacher trainers, we have huge responsibilities to shoulder. I will reiterate that fear as a tool to discipline is outdated, so if we create a culture of respect and appreciation, we will have more students who will choose to walk on an ethical path.

We used to discuss current affairs in the class. We used to watch documentaries surrounding global issues and sustainable development goals and engage in a dialogue about how we can build some solutions. If I would learn something interesting while doing my research work, I would take that to the classroom. I wanted my research to be useful and hence I always discussed it with my students. Teachers are actually always doing some or the other kind of research, they are just not reporting that research. They are always searching and analysing information, observing students and trying new things in their classroom and this is nothing but research. Me and my students together made efforts to bring new things to the class, sometimes it can be a quote, sometimes current affairs and sometimes an activity or a resource for teaching. We made sure that we become learners first, and then teachers because this is the only principle that can help us remain relevant in the field.

I also tried using the idea of differentiated learning in one of my classes. I had to take a demonstration class for the teachers. I chose the topic French revolution. Art and literature were two vital things in this revolution. So I decided to take poems, artwork, famous speeches and research as four different alternatives. All these resources presented the concept of revolution. I wanted students to understand the concept in-depth. So I divided the class into groups and students get to select the resource they want to work with. Based on their choice, they engage with the resource together, brainstorm and create a recipe of revolution. I had some wonderful recipes at the end of the class. Students enjoyed it and with a sense of affirmation they said, "we will also do similar lessons in our class."

I don't intend to boast. I am just sharing an activity. You can also try this in your class and you will see your students' faces lighting up with energy and smiles. I might not have done everything I wanted to but I am proud of two things. One, I was always there to listen to my students. I wanted to be an approachable teacher and I was always there for them. Students felt safe when they came and shared something with me. I tried to sort things out for them, I would also speak up for them. According to the system, I should not be on the students' side, but I was on their side and I am proud that I did so. Two, I experimented a lot. I tried taking something new to the class everytime and I definitely learnt a lot. This experience has made me a better educator, a better person.

It is good to have a class that is a little noisy, and not always quiet. There is no need to shut students down. There is no need to be strict with these students. We are past that era now. We cannot use fear as a tool to discipline anymore. If they love and respect their teachers, they will listen to their teachers. At the university level, don't tell students to not look out of the window and focus on the presentation. Let them look out of their windows, I am sure they are still listening to you. They will remember you if you can build a connection. They will not remember you if you throw your jargons at them and shut them down.

It has been two years since I formally taught my first batch of students. They still remember. We are all connected and we are a community of change makers. Before we ended our formal session of learning, I did a screening of the film Dead Poets Society with them outside of the classroom. That film tells a lot about how students are not allowed to think for themselves and made to follow tradition. That film gives an example of an extraordinary educator who stood against all odds for students. With that film we promised each other that we will always be committed to this passion for education, even if this means going against the system. Rather than sitting on some big chairs and becoming irrelevant, we decided to keep our spirits alive. As teachers we will consider ourselves as giants in the class, not the ones that dominate and impose rules, but the ones who can make a difference.

The experience and joy of teaching these students will always hold a special place in my heart. Whether it is academic class, or a dance class, I have always been blessed with student power and I am grateful for this. I could take some big steps in life because I was supported by students. Being a teacher is definitely the most rewarding experience. I couldn't have asked for more.

PhD- The Struggle Story

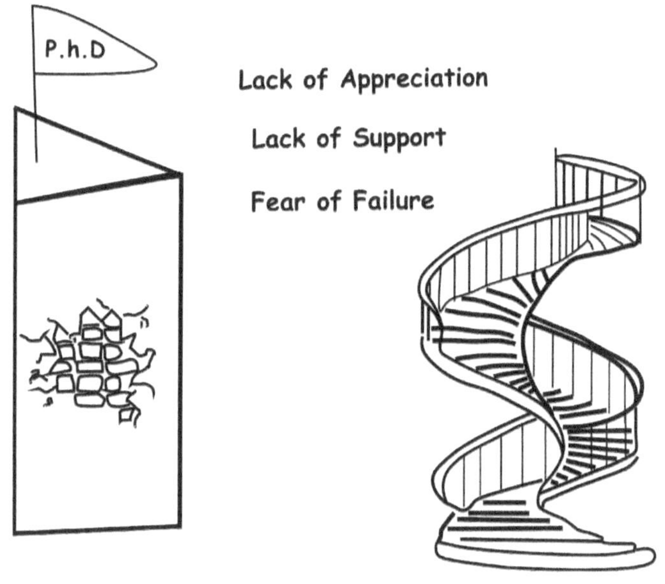

I entered the library, kept my stuff on my desk and started working on my laptop. I would usually go for a desk placed near the window. The cool breeze, the plants would help me feel good. A few moments later, I looked out of the window, I thought to myself, how confident that girl was- the only humanities student in her entire school and now she was so lost. I looked back at the document opened on the screen. The document was titled Methodology. I took a deep breath, tried writing a sentence and erased it again. Everyday I would enter with a feeling that maybe today I will be able to write something, I will be able to make some progress or I will get some response from the professors. But I didn't know how to proceed. I felt confused, I felt anxious and I felt clueless. I looked out of the window again, and it was raining. I wanted to shut down my laptop and run away. I was feeling exhausted because of being stuck at this one point for the last six months.

This was after 2 years of spending time on my PhD. I had never imagined things to get so challenging, so toxic. I was questioning my own worth as a researcher. Maybe, I don't know enough. But then I was here to learn right? And many PhD students are struggling, are they also not worth it? Are they also concerned about their future? I was here to learn. I was here to work. I was here to give my hundred percent. I was willing to refine things, and correct my work. But I didn't know what was wrong? What direction should I step in? Two years completed, and I felt like I was on borrowed time already.

I would keep waiting for emails, for responses from professors, from others who were supposed to validate my research tools. The wait seemed endless. It was easier to get a response from professors who worked outside India, but to get a response from someone in the university felt almost impossible. It is also a thing in Indian Academia, people don't really respond to emails, or they take a long time to show that they are super occupied. I must mention that there were a few helpful professors also, who stood by me throughout and supported me, and I am grateful for that. In this country, professors are busy doing their administrative work, and publishing their own articles. Ofcourse, only if they publish, they will survive, they will have a job. So publish publish publish, by hook or crook. Even if this means manipulating data, or paying a huge amount. It is disappointing to see that people don't write articles because they feel passionate about something, or they want to do some path-breaking research. They write articles only for the sake of publication.

Researchers are often pushed to publish and present their papers. They are constantly told to attend conferences and present papers. It is good to attend conferences and learn, connect with others, and build networks. It is good to present papers, it will help in enhancing the quality of research. But what kind of conferences should we go for? Most of these conferences I attended were so superficial, and so irrelevant. These conferences were nothing but tea parties. They would conduct conferences on the same old topics, and the same old people would come and read presentations. Students would attend these conferences like they would attend their regular classes. They would sit and listen to the lectures and that's it. I often felt that there was only little that we could learn from such conferences. And if researchers refuse to present papers in these in-house conferences, they will be questioned- "Where else do you think you will get to present if not in these conferences?" Today, I have certificates and credentials to answer this question. These events, workshops, and conferences should be so interesting, engaging and relevant for students. They should be able to target important current affairs of the field. These events hold immense potential for learning, only if they are done with a vision. But here they are done only for a tick mark on the checklist. They are done for certification. It is just a formality so that later on there are no issues with accreditation and getting the best grades for the university.

I was always a person who looked forward to events. I have learnt a lot from these events. Coordinating them and providing good experiences to everyone is something that I enjoy doing. I was told that I will be leading the conference of the department and I will be paid on an hourly basis for my contribution to the conference. I worked on this happily for one month and when the conference was just a week away, the authority told me that I will not be paid because some other higher authority has rejected the budget proposal. Research scholars need not be paid for the extra work they might be doing. This is just one example. There are many other such examples where we were told to work without getting paid. We keep contributing to their administrative requirements and eventually we get so tired that we don't have time and energy for our research work. If researchers take half a day off for their health, they are questioned.

We need to sit in front of these professors and help them finish their work. If I chose to sit in the library, that also was not acceptable. And If I wish to take unpaid leave also, I have to inform some ten people, because "Rajvi, there are some rules, regulations and systems in place and you need to follow those". They were least concerned about our experiences while pursuing PhD, all they bothered about was their rules and systems.

Since we are talking about payment, I must mention the difference in fees and stipend and the rules surrounding it. The stipend we received was quite low and it did not even provide us enough to cover some of the basic expenses. My stipend was based on my attendance. As researchers, even if we go for some other events related to our field, we have to lose the stipend for those days. Apart from this, if we got any opportunities to present our work outside India, the university would not support us in any way. Even when we were presenting papers somewhere, our stipend was cut and we were marked absent. So we must be present at the university all the time and not engage in something that was necessary for our research work. With regard to the fees, if we couldn't complete the PhD within a certain period of time, we had to pay triple the regular amount. Thankfully, I was able to survive, because of parental support and the amount I received through my dance classes. But think about other scholars, what would have been their condition? Imagine the fear of failure, the anxiety of not completing on time, and the difficulties faced by researchers. Only a handful of researchers will tell you that they did not have a tough time completing their research work.

Researchers who are always working for some senior professors can never say no to anything. We must learn the skill of saying yes to everything. Some professors would show off their expertise and their publications and they would advise research scholars to follow those articles only. Obviously, those articles would show us the right way of doing things. Those articles contain everything we need to know. When I went and shared my problems with these senior professors, they were reluctant. They would just not accept that there can be issues with the functioning of their department. They think their way of looking at things is the only right one and every other way is absolutely foolish. So they like people who say yes to everything, who can easily fit in, who will always work for them, and who don't have a voice of their own. The moment you stand up for yourself, it is a war between them and you. They will make your life so difficult that you will not be able to make any progress. This is how society and systems function right? If we shut up and keep following blindly, our lives will run smoothly. The moment we stand up for ourselves, we have to be prepared for the worst outcomes. Why do we always end up saying yes? Do we teach the next generation to say no? Look at corporate life, isn't it important that people learn to say no? Why do we have to put the seniors on a pedestal? Why are we never encouraged to question the wrong?

The space and culture was such that new ideas were not welcomed at all. The same old things and the same old processes would be retained. Any effort of doing something new and unique was ridiculed. It was a thing to be gossiped upon in the staff room. They are still stuck with redundant systems and red-tapism. You need a hundred approvals for a small little project of yours. After attending a number of faculty development programs, these professors couldn't even learn to listen to students without judgement and bias. In fact some of them feel that they are in such big positions, that they can't come down to "students' levels." They have already formed an image about students and labelled them. Instead of bridging that gap and building rapport, they say that they can't come down to "students' levels". I found it difficult to follow these people and survive in this culture.

However, I still wanted to do good work. I wanted to do a workshop for the students. I was not charging anything because this was a funded project. A resource person was joining online for this event. I was providing food, materials, and the entire experience free of cost. This module was specifically developed for trainee teachers with guidance from experts. It was not anything that I had picked up from the internet. It was well-researched and well-thought of. It included group activities, innovative learning approaches and things that would have helped teachers make their classrooms more engaging. When I presented this proposal, they made excuses. They kept delaying things. I waited for more than 3 months. Without even checking with the higher authorities, they declared that the authority had rejected my proposal. Because a budding researcher and teacher should not be encouraged to bring good things to the department. They were so insecure, that they did a whole lot of politics to keep me away from implementing my projects. I was no less. I made sure that I implemented all of those projects independently and I did not let go of my opportunities because of these professors. Me working on projects independently created huge chaos. Now, it was them against me, and they made sure I got no more opportunities, no more responses and I could make no more progress in my work. They also advised students to maintain a distance from me. It is a different thing that students never listened to that advice.

I left teaching. I felt that I should maintain a distance from the department so that I can focus on my research work. But, they did not like this too. Following were the questions asked-

If I went to my native after submitting my work to my guide, I would be asked- "With whose permission did I go home?"

If I am not seen in the department, I would be asked- "We have noticed your attendance. We know you are not available. Where have you been? Why are you sitting in the library?" They wanted to keep a close check on me and they wanted everything to be under their control. I couldn't tolerate this and I started feeling alienated. For six long months, I was only waiting for responses. There was not a single person on the campus who was concerned about the well-being of PhD students. There was not a single authority who would respond to my concerns and issues. There was no one who could be approached. At times, my parents would generally ask about my progress, and I would lose it. I would burst out into tears. I didn't have an answer to that question. My parents would also ask the same question. Can you not consult someone on campus? Did your professors respond to your emails? The guilt of not making any progress, not completing my work on time, was increasing day by day. I used to love my work, and now I was running away. I felt lost, I had no idea what to do. I was constantly questioning myself, blaming myself. What about my dreams? How will I complete my work in the next 6 months? If I don't complete, I need to ask for more financial help from my parents and I have to keep fighting in this setup. For how long will this struggle last? Should I quit?

I appeared to be strong on the outside, I was always fighting. I had my internal battles too. The institution had been successful in making me feel worthless. I was constantly worried about my career, my future. I still remember one day in the college cafe I was sitting and crying with my head down. I was trying to hide my tears. A lady figured it out and randomly told me that she knew how this place was. Though she managed to console me, she also said that she had faced similar issues. She did not have a choice but to say yes to everything her professors asked for. She just had to accept things. At that moment, I felt helpless. I was this person who used to feel empowered, and would often spread positive energy around. And now I was turning into this person who was filled with negativity, frustration and disappointment. I was turning into an escapist. People around me also observed this. It started to appear in my everyday behaviour. When someone is mentally so disturbed it is evident in their body language. Was this the beginning of my downfall? A gold medalist had lost it all? Will I ever be able to dream again? Will I ever be able to feel good about myself again? Will I be able to become the strong and independent person I always wanted to be? These were the daunting questions of that time.

It is exactly at this point that I received a wonderful opportunity to present my work at a symposium held at Soka University, Japan. I was sceptical about my work, my confidence but I still decided to go. I wasn't sure if I would be able to collect enough data and present it at the symposium but I tried. I was hopeful about this experience and I wanted to give it a shot. Though I got no support from the institution, I managed to gather data, and prepare the poster for presentation. I went there and this was my first international solo trip. I was already feeling better, and I made sure that I gave this my best shot. The symposium, the learning experience, the institution and the people everything was absolutely amazing. They were so welcoming. They appreciated me for my thoughts, for the vision behind the research work that I had taken up. I instantly connected with a lot of people there and we realised that we share similar thoughts in terms of how education needs some reforms. Although I couldn't completely keep aside the PhD story, I was feeling validated here. A lot of people said that I was doing good work and that created a huge impact. It helped me regain my strength and confidence. I could observe that at Soka university, they were actually practising ideas and not just preaching. They were transforming students' lives positively and I could see the energy radiating. Everyone was driven by passion, students did not attend the symposium for attendance or marks. They attended the symposium out of interest, curiosity and passion for learning. The entire trip helped me regain my confidence to an extent and made me feel empowered. For once, I had one response to all questions. I have done good work, and even if I drop my PhD I will still thrive in life, not just survive. I could probably do something creative, something of my own and I will still be happy. I don't really have to get this degree and get a job risking my mental health and mental peace. I have the ability to bounce back and I will do so.

When I got back from the trip, I had made up my mind that I was dropping my PhD. I would find ways of surviving. For one last time, I wanted to visit my university and meet my professors. I wanted to see their attitude and make a decision. It was the same. They did not even ask me about how I was doing, or how my presentation was. I had a conversation and I felt that probably they have accepted the system to such an extent that they will never be able to step out of it and think beyond. They will never be able to understand the struggles that I was facing. It is in this conversation that I followed my intuition and said, "This is it. We are done. I quit my PhD." I can't handle this anymore. There is no guarantee that things around will improve. There is no guarantee that I will find some direction in the near future. There is no guarantee that someone will guide me and help me in publishing my articles. There is no guarantee that someone will actually listen to me. I left no stone unturned. I reached out to authorities, I sent emails to every other authority concerned. No one even bothered. I don't know if they even read my emails. After two years they did send a letter mentioning I was not doing my work, and I needed to pay my fees if I wanted to continue. Reading that letter, I smiled and thought to myself, "good decision, Rajvi." After a few months, my students also told me, "Ma'am good you came out of that space. They don't deserve you". At this moment, while I write this chapter, I have no regrets in admitting that I dropped my PhD.

With this I want to ask one question- What makes a good institution? Those big buildings, the brand name and the accreditation documents- Are these enough to help you make a good institution? What about the culture of the university? What about the students? How often do you think about students when you make your policies? This institution had a whole system of faculty evaluation and feedback. But that entire thing was fake. Students' opinions were never taken seriously. This is for educational leaders everywhere. Please think about it. What makes a good institution? "A university is not the result of a system or a building programme but a product of the determination and passion of young people seeking new knowledge and wisdom...A university without eager students is a university without life, a university in which the main purpose has been forgotten". (Daisaku Ikeda, 2010)

I am writing this on behalf of all those PhD students who are facing issues, who are unable to make any progress for no fault of their own and who are unable to find ways. Through this book, I am urging you all to be considerate and sensitive to students' needs. We need to create systems that are actually meant for students and not those that claim to be student centred but are always demotivating students and shutting them down. If systems and institutions do not pay attention to students, then they will certainly become irrelevant. To those leaders and professors out there, please be more approachable and humble. If possible, add value to students' journeys and help them become better versions of themselves.

It took me a lot of courage to write this book, especially this chapter. But I did it. I accepted and admitted things. I am grateful for whatever happened. Yes, I am a proud PhD dropout. I have no regrets. I am happy that I said no to toxicity. I am glad that I am not a part of a highly commercialised system. I am grateful that I stepped out of the golden cage. I am happy that I chose mental peace and passion, over a degree. I am happy that I chose myself.

These experiences became the foundation for something bigger. This opened up some new doors and windows...

CHAPTER VII

Sattva- A Space for Lifelong Learning

45

After I dropped my PhD, I started applying for jobs. I explored a few job opportunities, but I was still unable to ignore those experiences at the university. I did not want to jump into another toxic system again. I was worried that I would not find the kind of work I wish to do. But with time I realised that I should rather work independently and I should give myself some time to carve my path. I was blessed to have a lot of parental support in this decision. My parents were with me through this entire process and they always told me to listen to my inner voice and get into the work that I would enjoy doing the most. My hobby, dancing, really helped me. It kept me sane. It also became the major source of earning for me. It gave me the confidence that I could be on my own. I am grateful that I kept pursuing my hobby throughout. I would participate in events, I would perform and I would take online and offline dance classes. If I have been able to achieve small milestones, it is because of dancing.

With such support and with positivity that my parents shared with me, I felt that I could do something of my own. I don't necessarily have to work for another organisation. Inspired by the workshops and events that I had conducted independently and the feedback received from my students, I felt that I could probably create a happy learning space for learners. I might not want to enter a formal learning set up. But one can teach and learn in any space, it doesn't have to be within the four walls of a classroom. I felt that I could actually build a community of changemakers. I always got a positive response from my students and that motivated me even more. I was good at building a rapport with students, and I don't have to let go of my dream or my passion. I just have to pursue it in a different way.

Let's go back to the questions we discussed in the very first chapter of this book. What is the purpose of education? What are the attributes that we want learners to acquire? Can we not make learning fun and engaging for everyone? Driven by these questions, I decided to create an informal learning space, titled Sattva- A Space for Lifelong Learning. I did not have a structure in mind then. Even now, it is tough to have a structure. Sattva has been and probably will always be about the process, the experience rather than the product, or the outcome. Remember the question about attendance? Yes, through Sattva I wanted to provide such a happy and engaging experience that learners feel like attending classes even when there is no rule of attendance.

At Sattva, we provide fun, creative, and transformative learning experiences for learners of all ages, abilities, and backgrounds. We encourage learners to explore their hidden potential and grow fully, becoming engaged local, national, and global citizens. The philosophy that was the foundation for my research work, was also the base for Sattva. The difference was that now I had walked past the need of having a degree. I started curating learning experiences and connecting with like-minded educators and aspiring change makers. I also kept learning alongside. I wouldn't miss any workshop, online course or programme that was relevant for me.

At Sattva - A Space for Lifelong Learning, we believe that education goes beyond acquiring degrees and jobs. We are committed to nurturing well-rounded individuals who are not only knowledgeable but also compassionate, creative, and engaged citizens. Our goal is to create a space that fosters lifelong learning and personal growth. Sattva reflects the dream of all revolutionary educators who wish to transform society and contribute to creating a better and sustainable world.

At Sattva, we would often take classes in cafes, in natural spaces, in parks and in artistic studios. We also made sure that we integrated art with education. I would often use dance, theatre and other art forms in my sessions with the youth and the kids. One of our engaging activities includes "dialogue on documentaries". In this session, we come together and watch some eye-opening documentaries surrounding global issues, and work in groups to arrive at some practical solutions to solve those problems. We are grateful for the support of SIMA Academy because they provided us a great platform where we found a lot of resources and good documentaries. Through this session, we enhance critical thinking and problem solving skills and we also try to make people more aware and sensitive. We received great response and appreciation for this event at Sattva. We also always made sure that we don't charge our learners, or we charge a minimal amount from them. The idea is not to commercialise and become a part of the system. We will always keep our experiences affordable and open for all. We have many other interesting modules for students and teachers. We try and cover important topics like digital literacy, collaboration, team work, empathy and others for students and innovative pedagogy and approaches in GCED for teachers.

Based on the projects conducted earlier, and the work done at Sattva, I also achieved a milestone. I was invited by Asia Pacific Centre of Education for International Understanding (APCEIU), UNESCO to one of their events- Advanced Alumni Forum. This was held in Seoul, South Korea in October 2023. This was one of the most beautiful, empowering and impactful learning experiences of my life. I was absolutely overjoyed to receive this invitation. I had participated in their events, online workshops and courses earlier and I always wanted to learn with them in-person. In this advanced forum, I got an opportunity to connect with educators and young change makers who were on a similar journey like me, and who were doing some exceptional work. I got a chance to meet some amazing mentors and facilitators who were so humble, so helpful and so supportive. Those facilitators radiated so much positivity in our sessions as well as in our conversations, that we felt really motivated and empowered. I shared my work with everyone and I received a lot of love and appreciation for the same. It has been a year to this experience but I still find it difficult to find the right words to express what I was feeling when I was there. It was after two years that I felt free. For once, I was not feeling trapped in guilt, I was not worrying about the future, I was not feeling stuck. For once, I had done away with self-doubt. I felt free and relieved and I heard that inner voice - "Rajvi, good work."

I wasn't feeling good because I had done some great work. Not at all. In fact when I went there I could see the tremendous amount of work others had done and I knew that I was taking only baby steps. I was feeling good because after a long time I felt that I was working in the right direction. I felt validated for my efforts. I realised that I wasn't just wasting time, energy and resources. I was actually doing important work. The mentors and friends who heard my story also empathised with me and said it takes courage to do what I did. It is in this journey that I got to perform at an educational conference. I presented a piece integrating art and education. I portrayed the issues of the education system from the perspective of 21st century learners through dance. I wrote the piece, recorded it and choreographed it as well. Through the piece, I wanted to urge educators and leaders to build a safe, engaging and empowering learning space for their students. I performed this piece, and received a lot of appreciation. People related to the piece, and they said that somewhere my performance created an impact. My father often told me that I am blessed with dancing skills, and it is through dancing that I will be able to reach greater heights, not through my gold medals or marks. He was right. My art helped me thrive during the toughest of times, and it is for this art that I was appreciated by people on a global platform. I will be grateful for this opportunity forever. That day, post performance, I felt so energised and empowered that I felt I could still make it. I don't have to give up on my dream, my passion or myself. I will find ways eventually. This journey was really fruitful in every possible way and gave me a fresh perspective for my work as well.

In this journey, I felt free and empowered. I felt heard, seen and valued for my work. It was for the very first time that I was anxious and scared about coming to my own country. I have always loved this country, and I have always wanted to work for India. Almost everyone told me that the kind of work I am doing, I must leave this country and settle abroad. We observe this often right. People are told to go and settle in other countries but why? I always argued with people and firmly mentioned that whatever it takes, I am going to work for this country. The trip to Seoul was so beautiful and fruitful, it made me realise that dreams can turn into reality. And I did not want to go back to that country where I have to keep fighting, keep struggling and keep justifying things. This feeling was making me feel so uncomfortable. Whatever happened in the past had created such an impact that I felt there was no point of going back. I wished the trip never ended.

We need to fight if we want to work on our own terms. We need to struggle if we want to do something different from the mainstream. We must establish ourselves based on the timelines decided by the society, if we are late we have to be prepared for various kinds of judgements. As women, we have to prove ourselves, if not we will be forced to be homemakers and we will have no choice, no say in anything. If we want to make decisions about our lives, we must be well established in terms of work and finances. If we are kind and polite, we won't survive in half of the places as everyone out there wants to take advantage and exploit people. If we are young and freshers in the field, we won't be given any opportunities. And above everything else, if we are budding artists, we won't ever be considered as people who are working, who have a job to do or people who have a respectable position in the society. There are so many people out there who want to stay here, who want to work for this country, and who wish to change things here for the good. But do they ever get any support? Are their efforts ever valued? Why do we have to go to another country for freedom and recognition? Why can't we change things here? If we can change things here, we might really solve the issue of brain drain. We might be able to use our demographic dividend for the good of our own country. In future, If I move out, I will do so only because I will be exhausted. The fight to live an independent and creative life will make me feel so exhausted that I will eventually give up and leave.

After I came back, I kept working on Sattva. I made efforts to make it better, and I kept improving and I added some new elements to it. I got some new opportunities, and I also had a community of change makers and like-minded people. We all wanted to contribute to a more peaceful and sustainable future together and we kept taking small little steps. Today, Sattva is not too big an organisation. It is not a big school. It is just another budding project and through this we are making best efforts possible to make this world brighter than it was. I believe that Sattva- A Space for Lifelong Learning will be remembered for transformative learning experiences, and the students here will turn into citizens who will have a similar urge for transformation like me. Through our events and actions, we will continue to reflect the dreams and hopes of educators.

The girl who confidently said that she will not succumb to the pressure, she will pursue humanities is going to be back in action. The girl who always loved dancing continues to dance and improve her work. The girl who struggled to accept herself is slowly smiling when she looks at her reflection now. The girl who cried, who fought and who was once helpless is now more confident about her work. She is not disheartened, she shows up everyday. She raises her voice for the good. She continues to spread the joy of learning. She has not given up, she still dreams, and she will continue to do so.

A Glimpse Of Our Journey!

Through Sattva, we have taken the initiative to develop humane, happy and student-focused learning spaces. We are delighted to share some images from our events and wish to spread an optimistic message. One can bring about a change, if there is a will to do so. Let us come together and educate for a better world.

Dialogue on Documentaries- Learning through eye-opening films!

We always add colours and activities to bring out the inner child!

No end to learning- We stepped into employee engagement programmes so that we could take global citizenship and transformative education to adults as well.. We deal with diverse age groups!

Discussions- We encourage dialogue so that students are open to existence of multiple perspectives.

Educators can create revolutions- An image from the screening of the film Dead Poets Society! The day we decided to follow passion, inner voice and the not the herd, or the system.

References

Academy of American Poets. (1913). The Road Not Taken. Poets.org. https://poets.org/poem/road-not-taken

Academy of American Poets. (1923). On Children. Poets.org. https://poets.org/poem/children-1

Birch, R. (2022, September 29). On bureaucracy. Rebecca Birch - On Education. https://rebeccabirch.substack.com/p/on-bureaucracy

Byker, J. E. (2016). Developing global citizenship consciousness: case studies of critical cosmopolitan theory. Journal of Research in Curriculum and Instruction, 20(3), 264 275.

Cain, S. (2012). Quiet: The power of introverts in a world that can't stop talking. Penguin Books.

Cline, B. (2024). Asking effective questions. (n.d.). Chicago Center for Teaching and

Learning | the University of Chicago. https://teaching.uchicago.edu/node/47

Commencement address by Martha C. Nussbaum | Colgate University. (n.d.). Colgate University. https://www.colgate.edu/news/stories/commencement-address-martha-c-nussbaum

Ikeda, D. (2010). Soka education: For the happiness of the individual. Middleway Press.

Kumar (2024). Suicides at IIT

https://www.business-standard.com/india-news/37-suicides-in-iits-since-2019-hyderabad-and-madras-highest-6-from-delhi-124060700767_1.html

LaMachia, J. (2016). Integrating Global Citizenship learning in Undergraduate Education. [Unpublished doctoral dissertation]. College of Professional Studies, Northeastern University

Magro, K. (2015). Teaching for Social Justice and Peace Education: Promising Pathways for Transformative Learning. Peace Research, 47, 109-141, https://www.jstor.org/stable/26382585

Ministry of Human Resource Development. (2020). National Education Policy 2020. Government of India. https://www.education.gov.in/sites/upload_files/mhrd/files/ NEP_Final_English_0.pdf

Orr, D. (2004) Earth in Mind- on education, environment and the human prospect. Washington: Island Press.

Phillips, Birgit & Phillips, Michael. (2020). Research Paradigms for Sustainable Development in Education: Critical reflective pedagogies for sustainable development and social transformation. 2-11.

Sterling, S. (2010). Transformative Learning and Sustainability: sketching the conceptual ground. Learning and Teaching in Higher Education, Issue, 5, 17-33.